INFORMED

INFORMED

Alison Stone

The New York Quarterly Foundation, Inc.
Beacon, New York

NYQ Books™ is an imprint of The New York Quarterly Foundation, Inc.

The New York Quarterly Foundation, Inc.
P. O. Box 470
Beacon, NY 12508

www.nyq.org

First Edition

Set in New Baskerville

Layout and Design by Raymond P. Hammond

Cover Painting: V. Perry Stone

Library of Congress Control Number:

ISBN: 978-1-63045-107-3

In Memory of my grandparents,
Perry and Jeanne Stone and Yale and Janet Cohn

Contents

Part 2

Part 3

Part 4

Part 1

Visit

Wherever you're going, you won't get there,
an owl's hoot warns small, scurrying beasts.
The moon is telling riddles tonight.
Insomniacs twist in their sheets.

The owl's hoot warns small, scurrying beasts,
There's more to fear than to praise.
Insomniacs twist in their sheets.
Sidewalks are littered with shriveling petals.

There's more to fear than to praise,
though I didn't know this when we kissed
on sidewalks littered with shriveling petals.
The virus blooming in your blood.

I didn't know when we kissed
that our future had fluorescent hospice light.
The virus bloomed in your blood.
You visit, then leave me, in dreams.

The moon is telling riddles tonight.
In fluorescent hospice light,
you whisper before leaving my dream,
Wherever you're going, you won't get there.

Party

We grasp our glasses tightly.
Wine and secrets are easy to spill.
Is everyone hungry?
The chanteuse looks ill.

Wine and secrets are easy to spill.
Both stain what they touch.
The chanteuse looks ill,
keens with pained sincerity.

Some words stain what they touch.
Held-in secrets and desires
keen. With pained sincerity
guests ask each other questions,

hint at secrets and desires,
scan the dimly-lit faces
seeking answer to the question
Will we be pariahed, or kissed?

Scan the dimly-lit faces.
Everyone is hungry.
Waiting to be pariahed or kissed,
we grasp our glasses tightly.

Picket Fence

The mother drinks in secret.
The father punches his shame into a wall.
So many ways to pretend.
The daughter hides beneath blankets.

The father punches his shame into a wall.
How did love end up like this?
The daughter hides beneath blankets
as the TV blares fake mirth.

How did love end up like this,
dinner finishing in tears
as the TV blares fake mirth?
In pictures, they all smile.

Dinners finish in tears,
though everything's wiped clean.
In pictures, they all smile
on beaches or the front lawn.

Everything's wiped clean.
The neighbors will never know.
On beaches or the front lawn
they're a typical family.

The neighbors must never know.
So many ways to pretend
they're a typical family.
The mother drinks in secrets.

Weeds

One is silver and the other gold.
Lined up by height, we sang what we were told.
There wasn't enough room, enough light.
Who was expendable? Who mattered?

Lined up by height, we sang what we were told.
The pretty and powerful taught us
who was expendable, who mattered.
To be desirable was to be safe.

The pretty and powerful teach us –
Cute endangered animals get more protection.
To be desirable is to be safe.
Some plants we poison, some tend.

Cute endangered animals get more protection.
There's not enough room, enough light.
Some plants we poison, some tend.
Milkweed silver, dandelion gold.

Time Pantoum

Time will pass, will you?
our teacher asked if we clock watched,
oblivious to the lesson.
Fidgeting, yearning to be elsewhere.

Our teacher said if we clock watched,
didn't learn, our futures would shrink.
We fidgeted, yearning to be elsewhere.
What did books know that we didn't?

We didn't learn our futures would shrink
until we graduated, married disappointment.
Books knew what we didn't –
that dreams were smoke and forever only for songs.

Until we graduated, married disappointment,
we kissed like kisses could save us.
That dream was smoke, forever only for songs.
Lines on our faces deepened.

We kissed like kisses could save us
under magnolias older than we'd ever be.
Lines on our faces deepened.
Our bones hungered for earth.

Under magnolias older than we'd ever be,
we kissed, oblivious to the lesson.
Our bones hungered for earth.
Time would pass, and so would we.

Teen Pantoum

I felt awkward everywhere,
my life unspooling like a film
where midnight offered, *Reinvent yourself.*
Frank-N-Furter pursed bright purple lips.

In the unspooling film,
(not a woman but dressed like a slutty one)
Frank-N-Furter pursed bright purple lips.
We sang along to every word.

Not a woman yet but dressed like a slutty one,
I obeyed when Joey urged, *Hey ho, let's go.*
We sang along to every word.
Sex was unfun, not what I expected.

I obeyed when Joey urged, *Hey ho, let's go.*
The boys were selfish or clumsy.
Sex was unfun, but expected.
It made you seem cooler.

Boys got selfish or clumsy
as the night ended, but they claimed us,
which made us seem cooler.
What we took into our bodies!

As the night ended, boys claimed us
with penises and false promises,
which we took into our bodies.
We woke cotton-mouthed, tired

of penises and false promises.
It's alright for some, innit?
Waking cotton-mouthed and tired,
my British boyfriend spat class rage.

It's alright for some, innit?
As a limo rolled its privilege by,
my British boyfriend spat. Class, rage,
where did I fit in?

A limo rolled its privilege by.
I wasn't rich like the ruling girls at school,
(Where did I fit in?)
nor street smart like my nightclub friends.

I wasn't rich like the ruling girls at school.
Though midnight offered, *Reinvent yourself,*
I couldn't swagger like my nightclub friends.
Felt awkward everywhere.

Learning

Somehow most of us survived
bus rides without seatbelts, monkey bars over blacktop,
failed tests, injuries in gym.
Lardo! Chris Piss wears girl's pants!

Bus rides without seatbelts, monkey bars over blacktop.
Cruelty served with Sloppy Joes and fruit cups –
Lardo! Chris Piss wears girl's pants!
Each of us learning how much space to claim.

Cruelty served with Sloppy Joes and fruit cups.
Five on one, books slammed to the ground.
Each of us learned how much space to claim,
who had the right to speak.

Five on one, books slammed to the ground.
We saw but never told.
Who had the right to speak?
Jill got hit by a car and died.

We saw (but never talked about)
Mr. Jones look down girls' shirts.
Jill got hit by a car and died.
What we didn't say lodged in our bodies.

Mr. Jones looked down girls' shirts,
Keith broke Sarah's nose in gym.
Though what we couldn't say lodged in our bodies,
somehow most of us survived.

Rocky Horror Pantoum

Don't dream it, be it, Frankie crooned.
Not cool enough for Columbia, I played Janet,
though after midnight, everything seemed possible.
I spent much of the show in a bra and slip.

Not cool enough for Columbia, I played Janet.
I was younger than everyone else
but spent much of the show in a bra and slip.
Smell of greasepaint, rhinestones' gleam.

I was younger than everyone else.
Some of them were in college, studying drama.
We smelled of greasepaint. Rhinestones gleamed.
Fishnet stockings crosshatched our legs.

Some of them were studying drama –
breakups, betrayals, accidents.
Fishnet stockings crosshatched our legs.
We all made out with each other.

Breakups, betrayals, accidents.
Paul traded his jeans for my sequined pants.
We all made out with each other.
Paul gave me poppers between scenes.

Paul traded his jeans for my sequined pants.
Did he know I fancied him?
He gave me poppers between scenes.
I read the love note in his pocket.

Did Paul know I fancied him?
Though dating the boy who played Brad,
I read the love note in Paul's pocket,
wanted what I couldn't have.

I was dating the boy who played Brad,
but nothing felt as real as our time onstage.
Wanting what I couldn't have,
I filled journals with pages of yearning.

Nothing felt as real as our time onstage,
confusing our characters with our selves.
My journals were pages of yearning.
Frankie promised absolute pleasure.

We confused our characters with our selves,
Don't dream it, be it, our mantra.
Frankie promised absolute pleasure.
After midnight, everything was possible.

Romance

We're dumb, dizzy. Smug with love.
Flushed faces, eager fingers.
The landscape's festive with flags.
We pray it will never end.

Flushed faces, eager fingers.
Who needs deep conversation?
We pray they'll never end,
these days shiny as our spent bodies.

Who needs deep conversation
when there are so many orgasms?
Shiny as our spent bodies,
fantasies and expectations feed.

When there are so many orgasms,
the mind doesn't know what it knows.
Fantasies and expectations feed.
Misgivings can be smothered like kittens.

The mind doesn't know what it knows,
though the landscape's lousy with red flags.
Misgivings smothered like kittens,
we're dumb, dizzy, drugged with love.

Inspired by a Line from Janis

Tired eyes, slack skin –
I swore I'd never get a face like my parents'
or spread their martyred, blame-filled love.
When did I break my vow?

I swore I'd never get a face like my parents' –
would sing loud and hunger with my whole heart.
When did I break my vow?
When did days take on a stain of disappointment?

I sang loud and hungered with my whole heart,
until I didn't,
and days got stained with disappointment.
Other people's needs a cloak of lead,

until I didn't
remember what freedom felt like.
Other people's needs a cloak of lead
I can't find a way to take off.

> *Remember freedom.*
> *More than nothing's left. Lose*
> *the martyred, blame-filled love,*
> *Shine in your slack skin.*

The Only

Sometimes the only hand to hold is your own.
When your joke's funny, laugh out loud.
If you are afraid of loneliness, Chekhov warned,
don't marry. The ring gleams.

When your joke's funny, laugh out loud.
Enough noise is given to lamenting.
Don't get married, despite the ring's gleam,
unless you can feel rage without acting.

Enough noise is given to lamenting –
Something's always lost or dead or out of reach.
Unless you can feel rage without acting,
try an isolated cabin in the woods.

Something's always lost or dead or out of reach.
If you are afraid of loneliness,
try an isolated cabin in the woods.
Sometimes the only hand to hold is your own.

Alexandre Cabanel's "Echo" (oil on canvas)

What would she say if she could speak?
Her world's reduced to light-splashed rock.
Her eyes are wide with terror or rage.
Sheer cloth barely covers her crotch.

Her world reduced to light-splashed rock.
Hands raised – to draw sound in or keep it out?
Sheer cloth barely covers her crotch.
In the myth, she wastes away for love.

Hands raised – to draw sound in or keep it out?
There's no shortage of men who love their voices.
In the myth, she wastes away for love.
Here her body's solid, fed by something we can't see.

No shortage of men who love their voices,
though right now she's alone,
her body solid, fed by something we can't see.
A veil covers her hair but not her face.

Right now she's alone.
Words circle inside her like trapped bees.
A veil covers her hair but not her face.
There were truths she knew but didn't tell.

Words circle inside her like trapped bees.
Her eyes are wide with terror or rage.
There were truths she knew but didn't tell,
what she'd say now if she could speak.

Sometimes the Eyes are Enough

What a woman knows, she tells slant.
Let men and the sun spill everything.
The moon, too, keeps secrets.
Birds broadcast their news all day.

Let men and the sun spill everything,
boast with bold voices and sharp light.
Birds broadcast their news all day –
romance, danger, squabbles for food.

Boasting with bold voices and sharp light,
the gods tell and retell stories
of romance, danger, squabbles for power.
Even our sweetest prayers are tinged with fear.

The gods write and revise stories,
humans cast in the supporting roles,
even our sweetest prayers tinged with fear.
The subjugated grow crafty with codes.

Cast in a supporting role,
the moon keeps silver secrets.
The subjugated grow crafty with codes.
What a woman knows, she tells slant.

Scholars Say

Eve didn't sin by tasting apple.
It was a pomegranate – thick-skinned globe
with ruby juice of pleasure and hell.
Woman, fruit – we've seen this myth before.

It was a pomegranate, thick-skinned globe
the snake pointed his forked tongue toward.
Woman, fruit – we've seen this myth before.
Persephone took seeds from Hades' hand.

The snake pointed his forked tongue toward
knowledge. Or was it nakedness?
Persephone took seeds from Hades' hand.
A girl's gotta grow up some time.

Knowledge, (or is it nakedness)
children learn, is tinted with shame.
A girl's gotta grow up some time,
though what's lost leaves scars.

Children learn – tinged with shame,
bodies can't be escaped, nor hunger.
What's lost leaves scars.
We create a god to give grief meaning.

Bodies can't be escaped, nor hunger
for the ruby juice of pleasure. Hell
we create, and God to give grief meaning.
Eve didn't sin by tasting apple.

Garden

Anemones bright with Adonis's blood,
reflection of narcissi in the pond –
myth offers structure for our heart's garden.
Crows nest in a fire-scorched oak.

Reflection of narcissi in the pond –
Is their beauty real or an illusion?
Crows nest in a fire-scorched oak.
Happy shrieks of children in the breeze.

Which beauty's real, which an illusion?
I lie in dying grass, gaze at the clouds,
hear happy shrieks of children in the breeze.
Another birthday without my mother.

I lie in dying grass, gaze at the clouds.
Words mean more than the dictionary lets on.
Another birthday without my mother.
Losses stack on each other like blocks.

Words mean more than the dictionary lets on.
A gesture, or its absence, changes everything.
Losses stack on each other like blocks.
Are dead loves transformed into stars?

A gesture, or its absence, changes everything.
Myth offers structure for our heart's garden –
dead loves transformed into stars,
anemones bright with Adonis's blood.

Why Don't We

The animals want us to go –
parrots, pumas, long-lashed giraffes.
Our greed limitless as stars.
Jewel-winged bugs buzz off into extinction.

Parrots, pumas, long-lashed giraffes.
What's lost won't be returned.
Jewel-winged bugs buzz off into extinction.
We couldn't keep our ruin to ourselves.

What's lost won't be returned,
like the true beat of our own hearts. Grabbing,
poisoning, we couldn't keep our ruin to ourselves,
though we're made from stardust, yearn for light.

Our poisoned hearts beat, *Grab more,*
greed limitless as the stars
we're made from. Too late for light.
The animals need us to go.

December

My neighbors' arguments are loud tonight –
rough, monotonous music.
Bright city lights obscure the stars.
The wind is undecided.

History's rough, monotonous music –
Blood and soil. Germany, Charlottesville.
The future's undecided.
The past is a constricting hug.

Blood and soil. Germany, Charlottesville –
newscasters have a lot to say.
The past is a constricting hug.
The moon's an eye, wide open.

Newscasters have a lot to say –
Poverty trickles down more easily than wealth.
The moon's an eye forced open.
Can we untie memory from regret?

Poverty trickles down easily,
thick and stubborn as the rope
tying memory to regret.
Now's a good time for a savior.

A thick, stubborn rope
of city lights obscures the stars.

Charlottesville Pantoum

If you're not outraged, you're not paying attention,
Heather Heyer posts. (Her last post)
The president blows his dog whistle.
Unite the Right flyers don't mention the statue.

Heather Heyer posts her last post.
Counter-protestors make signs.
Unite the Right flyers don't mention the statue
of General Lee looking down from his horse.

Counter-protestors bring signs.
The Right bring torches, guns, and shields.
General Lee looks down from his horse
at swastikas and Confederate flags.

The Right have torches, guns, and shields,
chant *Jews will not replace us,*
wave swastikas and Confederate flags.
Some very fine people

chant *Jews will not replace us.*
The president says, (No more dog whistles)
some very fine people.
If you're not outraged, you're not paying attention.

I Will Celebrate, Even So

The news, as usual, is full of woe.
Hatred spreads like mushrooms after rain.
The earth's too hot and getting hotter.
In Paris, history and beauty burn.

Hatred spreads like mushrooms after rain.
The dead I love remain gone.
In Paris, history and beauty burn.
The landscape explodes into spring.

The dead I love remain gone.
One grievance follows another
despite the land's explosion into spring –
young shoots, sunlit river, marigold.

Grievances follow one another.
The news, as usual, is full of woe.
Still, the young shoots, sunlit river, marigold.
My long marriage hot and getting hotter.

How Louisa May Alcott is Similar to God

Best behavior only lasts so long.
Who you date is never who you marry.
Still, all heart wounds look the same in the dark.
Love, like mothering, succeeds if *good enough.*

Who you date is never who you marry.
In *Little Women,* Laurie switches sisters.
Love, like mothering, succeeds when *good enough.*
Each relationship brings its frustrations.

In the bible, Rachel's father switches sisters –
Leah's unloved face beneath the veil.
Each relationship brings its frustrations.
After seven years, Jacob gets a new bride.

Poor Leah, unloved beneath the veil.
The wrong spouse, a stand-in for a fantasy.
After seven years, Jacob gets a new bride.
What do vows mean, really?

Since each spouse is a stand-in for a fantasy,
what do vows mean, really?
Best behavior only lasts so long.
All heart wounds look the same in the dark.

Louder than Laughter

Dead lovers are the hardest to forget.
The thing you stopped yourself from saying echoes.
Those long-gone reach out as wind on skin.
Our bodies form from memory and stardust.

The thing you stopped yourself from saying echoes
louder than laughter or waves.
Our bodies formed from memory and stardust,
we're jerked from desire to desire.

Louder than laughter or waves,
our grievances and hungers mutter.
We're jerked from desire to desire
as the moon lessens then swells.

Grievances and hungers mutter.
We inhale the past with every breath.
The moon lessens then swells,
draws the night animals from their lairs.

We inhale the past with every breath.
Snapped twigs and crunching leaves
draw the night animals from their lairs.
Often what seems finished isn't.

Snapped twigs, crunching leaves,
soft wind on skin – those long-gone reach out.
Often what seems finished isn't.
Dead lovers are the hardest to forget.

Cargo

Everywhere I go, I take my dead.
Mom would have loved Rome,
the masterpieces and churches.
Religions stacked on top of each other.

Mom would have loved Rome,
though Grandma was afraid to fly.
Religions stack platitudes on top of each other
but can't bring back her Yiddish curses.

Grandma was afraid to fly –
She'd make a terrible angel.
No place in heaven for Yiddish curses,
and the music's always the same.

Those I loved would make terrible angels –
Jay with his sea-blue eyes and prison tats,
the music he blasted always the same,
top down, cruising back roads.

Jay with his sea-blue eyes and prison tats
travels with my friends and relatives,
top down, cruising back roads.
A whole crew I won't let go of.

I travel with my friends and relatives
past masterpieces and churches.
This whole crew I won't let go of.
Everywhere I go, I take my dead.

Part 2

Yourself

The sweet, soul-killing lies you tell yourself.
No need for Satan – You build Hell yourself.

Bravado of storm clouds slicing the moon.
You mocked the love-struck till you fell yourself.

Dad's sex advice – *A man won't buy the cow*
if he gets free milk. Don't give, sell yourself.

Brew of wolfsbane, mugwort, and tears. No need
to call a priestess. Cast the spell yourself.

Anger turns sour, fear locks all the doors.
Love opens the cold, cramped cell of yourself.

Beneath the pond's surface – insects, trout. What's
reflected in the mirror or well – your self

or a protective mask? Burn incense,
sit down. When you meditate well, your self

melts to ego-free joy. If welcomed, you
thrive. If put-down, you learn to quell yourself.

Screw beauty, Alison. Spend energy
elsewhere. Enough to not repel yourself.

Like the Night

He chose friends for wit, his bride for beauty.
She always erred on the side of beauty.

Punk soul in a Father's body, Hopkins
wrote the motley an anthem – *Pied Beauty*.

Mary Oliver's speaker walks with awe
through the world. Dickinson's died for beauty.

From the inside. Eye of the beholder.
Well-meaning parents lied about beauty.

Shooting star, marigold, peacock's jeweled tail.
The cop lets the hot speeder slide, beauty

a higher law. Are we happy for friends'
luck, or do we envy wealth, pride, beauty?

Awed by her fine-boned face and lanky frame,
we reeled from Liz's suicide, beauty

failing as an antidote to despair.
Add break-up, no job. Divide by beauty.

Still sexy at sixty-four, Adam Ant
claims the stage with a young stud's stride. Beauty

indelible as memories of our teen
selves, school ruled by surly jock, snide beauty.

Kids think their grandparents were always old.
Too soon, our own faces slide from beauty

to ghost. Stone, remember all the wasted
time? Young, lovely, dumb, you cried for beauty.

Sorrowful Ghazal

AM radio broadcasts trite sorrow.
A too-long marriage – strained meals, spite, sorrow.

The thin moon's silver blade cuts deep. Moss spreads
fluffy green erasure. Tonight, sorrow

commands the landscape. Everywhere, rotting
trees. Stray bones and tufts of fur. Blight. Sorrow.

The table laid, the right wine chosen. At
six he welcomes guests. At midnight, sorrow.

Raised fists and ugly signs hide separation's
pain. Under white bigotry, white sorrow.

What you attend to grows, the book warns. *Do
you focus on joy or highlight sorrow?*

Mother-scarred, he gives his heroines cads
for boyfriends, harmful appetites, sorrow.

Raindrops blur a chalk version of Starry
Night, while coffee-house kids recite sorrow-

heavy poems. For a pity party,
serve warm beer in smudged mugs. Invite sorrow.

The ivy's rioting – suffocating
shrubs, choking the oak. At twilight, sorrow

presses down. I unwind the vines from my
daughter's birth tree, its bark stripped. Might sorrow

teach us something we can't learn another
way? Cats stalk mice. Chasing delight, sorrow.

Ghosts are souls who don't know life's over. They
float moaning from desire, fright, sorrow.

The nameless poet knows death always wins,
but she gives words to love, despite sorrow.

Lost Ghazal

Midnight. Teens wander – beautiful, lit, lost.
A homeless man waves his torn flag. *Git lost.*

How close lie pleasure and oblivion.
Till Roe – missed period, dead rabbit, lost

future. The waning moon makes her wonder
about old boyfriends – cop, convict, Brit. Lost

to time or wives. Renunciates fear their
hungers. The grump toasts, *Here's to more shit lost.*

The woman pulled to pieces by her kids' and
husband's needs. She offers kiss, toy, tit. Lost,

the free, whole self she once was. Moonlight turns
spilled blood black. Near porch lamps, doomed moths flit. Lost

dogs whine. The young obsess about death but
can't fathom their own bodies, looks, wit lost.

Satan's not your oo-woo angsty boy, one
goth tells another. We must admit – Lost

dreams don't come back. Watch the mom beg, *Tell me
where you've been,* and her dull-eyed son spit, *Lost.*

I want to die fully spent, each heart-stone
turned. Dissatisfaction, that culprit, lost.

Time

Quarantine. The pets get no alone time.
We can't stop its damage, why bemoan time?

I love the o's in *Oh Ghost most holy,*
Kali's necklace of skulls, Buddha's stone, time-

less grin. Burn herbs to match the moon's guises.
Learn hope from the Maiden. From the Crone, time.

My neighbor's confused rooster crows at noon.
Cause of death, chiseled on the gravestone, *time.*

Something so fast in the grass, I doubt my
eyes but not my heart's shiver. I'm shown, time

and again, the constriction of gender.
The girl's gift, dolls. The boy's, a trombone. Time

for earplugs and envy. Persephone
gets fruit, a hot husband, her own throne, time

away from Mom. Hell has its perks. Earth smells
like longing, with an undertone of time.

What does desire get us after all?
Our dreams are flimsy houses, blown by time.

Med students, after a thirty-hour
shift, raise a glass to life, a bone to time.

Remember sand beneath us on the beach?
How full and close the moon? How we shone? Time

irrelevant. Full of teen arrogance,
we thought we'd found a way to postpone time.

Do the dead really float in some better
realm – carefree, happy to have outgrown time?

Nothing's yours, Alison. Not those you love
best. Even this body's on loan from time.

Yellow Circle   Helios   Great Ball of Gas

Spooning, our dog and cat doze in the sun.
Tails twitch and amber eyes close in the sun.

Each dawn, the illusion of another
chance. Every evening Nut swallows the sun.

Poetry blooms in the moon's milky beams.
Drama in bedroom or bar light. Prose, the sun.

The sickle moon readies herself to rise.
Staining our faces pink, there goes the sun.

We're green, green sugar machines, kids dressed as
plants sing. Two fat squirrels pose in the sun.

Demoted from god to science project.
Stippling the leaves, warming our toes, the sun

keeps its bright eye open, rises and sets
expectedly, despite our woes – the son

a runaway, the daughter lost to dream.
Would you choose gifts the dark bestows? The sun?

Curved blade of a back alley moon. Shadows
fight, then mate. A caged rooster crows. The sun

lifts over the smog-thick city. Homeless
men sift through garbage. Brisk wind blows the sun-

streaked leaves. An old woman paints the park – stone
fountain, oak trees, bees in the primrose, sun.

Well-Lit

The groom donned cowboy boots, the bride wore light.
Spring blares its edict – The world needs more light.

Beauty's a cage women fight to stay in.
The cat bats a mouse. Noon sun's a bore, light,

like virtue, tiresome in its brightness.
Even Lucifer soured on splendor, light.

The first crimson leaves splotch lawns. Mourners rise
to guide beloved souls toward savior, light.

I fell arse over tits for a British
drummer, his leather pants, gray pallor. Light

changed to song by his sticks. Sex is debt both
bodies build, then pay. Victim/captor, light-

drenched tangled limbs. There are places folks don't
come back from, acts that close the door to light.

Shoots of wild onion. My hands take on
their tang when I unearth the bulbs. Poor light-

filled, unwanted things, consigned to compost.
The full moon paints the pond with donor light.

No protection from bullets in temples
or mosques. Maybe God's just metaphor, light

making the bush blaze. Turner brought prayer
to canvas, urged viewers to explore light.

Human nature to divide *us* from *them*.
Like solar panels, do angels store light?

Too easy, Stone, to despair in the dark.
Write swing-state postcards, work to restore light.

April Ghazal

Lawns hedged with forsythia's gold in spring.
Sun stronger but his heart stayed cold in spring.

Walkers and cyclists vie for space. Finding
something foul, Cadence sniffed, then rolled. In spring

the puppy in her rises up, despite
her muzzle's gray. She's hard to hold in spring.

Bodies propelled by throbbing drums to dance.
People and things that can't be controlled – Spring,

Corona virus, quarantined toddlers.
We watch the pandemic unfold. In spring,

she eats outside beneath an ombre sky.
Abundance of blues to behold in spring.

Full-bloom cherry and magnolia trees' brief
splendor. Your beauty never gets old, Spring.

Let your life's constraints melt off like snow. Speak
truth loudly, Alison. Grow bold with spring.

Home to Roost

I'm energized by animals, kale, song.
Our new cat named for a Nine Inch Nails song.

So much heart-breaking music – Garland's drug-
fueled rainbow, Billie's blues, Joplin's wail-song.

Bay of hounds chained in dusty yards. War chant.
Lament of the cancer-stricken. Jail song.

How to give the spirit voice? When fasting's
not enough, try sex. When words fail, song.

Bathtub-born, Sasha slipped from his mother
into water. In the background, whale song.

Jacob fooled his father. Karma wrote his
son an impostor-beneath-the-veil song.

History's chickens home to roost. Poe knew –
we're all exposed by the heart's telltale song.

In my dream, I drift from field to forest,
hear, through silver branches, wind's pale song.

Wrens have my mother's eyes. Her last concert,
Whitney missed the high notes. Shaky, frail song,

sound refusing to soar. Is this what killed
her, this broken promise, betrayal song?

Bombs, smog, greed, guns, oil-coated seagulls,
melting ice. We're all bored with that stale song.

Though it can be hard to love the world, find and
inhale beauty, Alison. Exhale song.

Into the Woods

Hope sparked by a bright field. Sorrow, the woods.
We caution children, *Don't go in the woods.*

The old knight survived three fire-breathing
dragons. Was felled by a foe in the woods.

The sun's reborn during the longest night.
Though Frost's iambs tell us, in snow, *the woods*

are lovely, dark, and deep, predators keep
their own promises. Eyes glow in the woods.

On the blue onesie, a Superman *S.*
On the pink, *I Hate My Thighs.* Oh, the woods

are full of monsters but our homes hold more.
The news repeats its tale of woe – the woods,

the blood-stained glove. Years safe, still Hansel and
Gretel live in the shadow of the woods.

How many married years before I learn
your body the way my dogs know the woods?

Sharks never sleep. The rapist scans the nightclub. Hunters track a wounded doe. The woods

thicken as sunlight fades. In dreams, Stone flies
then plummets to the world below the woods.

Memory

The shame, the clench, the slap of memory.
Years wasted in the trap of memory.

Odors of pine and rain-soaked earth tug at
the seal, start to unwrap a memory.

New haircut, strange town, sunny apartment.
At the window, the tap of memory.

His childhood an erased board. He can't
retrieve even a scrap of memory.

Hapless ghosts! Kept from oblivion,
yoked to earth by the strap of memory.

Palimpsest of bodies, lips, desires.
Present loves overlap with memory.

Children grown and gone. Husband *working late.*
Each evening – TV, nightcap, memory.

Her soft-spoken, loving parents beckon,
ageless in the gap between memory

and dream. Youth's bright colors still blaze. Let's raise
a glass or tip a cap to memory.

In Hell did Proserpine befriend the dead
and settle in Pluto's lap, memory

of green fading like ink? Yiddish curses,
Woolworth stools, a chocolate frappe – memory

brings Grandma back. *Write a real poem, Ali.*
Not unmetered pap about memory.

Monsters, Bees, Desires

The boy fears monsters, things that creep at night.
Beds half-empty, the widows weep at night.

I walk with my mother through a moonlit
town only accessible in sleep. Night

holds its prisoners tight. He drank and watched
the darkness dissipate. Fickle, cheap night.

Dawn. The sun begins its dazzle. Alarms
yank dreamers out of dreams. Birds' wings sweep night

from yards. She embraces sweatpants, pony-
tails, gray hair. Cool took too much upkeep – night

after night of eyeliner and witty
retorts. If you sow shadow, you'll reap night.

Sharp words from the morning hover like bees.
The day's unmet desires seep into night.

Teen years spent following the punk bands' beat.
Makeup like war paint, we'd leap into night.

The air chills. Sunset's pinks splash on the sky.
Long, thin river's cold, the mountain steep. Night

doesn't fall, it rises – thick and pulsing.
His inhibitions burrow deep at night.

The cat on Stone's chest stretches. So many
shelves for climbing, why stay asleep at night?

Enough about You

Sweet, eager, shy tech geeks wined and dined me.
The cute traffic cop flirted, then fined me.

Cravings wake under a cloud-veiled moon.
Chamomile and a lap cat unwind me.

Punchline Jewish mother bleeding in a
dark room. *Go out, have fun, Dear. Don't mind me.*

Before death's new initials, young, dumb, and
in love, sliced by nightclub light, we shined – me

blue-haired, Jay inked with coiled snakes. Emo
kids in a pack on the corner remind me.

Staid corporate days stack up like dirty plates.
The boss stole my idea then maligned me.

Night insects drowned out by a howling
bloodhound. Buffed and polished egos blind me.

Crackle of static on the vinyl disc.
Garland sang, *the clouds are far behind me,*

but they weren't. A pill for thin, a pill
for sweet half-sleep. Who says life is kind? *Me,*

too – so many women speak out, but to what
end? For years, men's judgments defined me.

On holidays, long lonely days, in our
shared birthday month, I want to rewind – me

cushioned by taken-for-granted mother
love. Her alive. In dreams she can't find me.

My daughter channels Williams. *This note's to
say I took your rings. They sparkle.* Signed, Me.

Gold frames hold old Alisons – newborn, pig-
tailed, sulky teen. Young, muscled, unlined me.

Just Emotion?

Virus. The government orders: Stay home.
Across highways, the cat made her way home.

To every season, a drink. With vodka,
we toasted nightclub nights. Chardonnay, home.

Counters scrubbed, rage locked away, pillows fluffed.
Food served. Our best moods on display. Home

sweeter for outsiders' eyes. Every mom,
at least once, wants to run away from home.

Odysseus kissed Penelope in
dreams. Her plain, faithful face – a ray of home.

In each family, something's forbidden – tears,
doubting God, hating sports, being gay. *Home*

is just emotion, Lene sang, *sticking
in my throat.* Children chant, *Fly away home,*

your house is on fire. Forget Engagement
Chicken – Love's nose-led. On pulse-points, spray Home.

What kind of god's too impatient to wait
for the school day to be done? Pray at home!

TV all day if she wanted. Mom at
the end of a bell. Snacks on a tray – Home

sick had perks. She wrote about this, not Dad's
temper, when assigned an essay on Home.

Quarantined, I thought I'd dream of Spain but
night brings well-known trees, the stone walkway home.

Tactile Ghazal

Locked down with family, I'm blessed with touch.
For some autistics, pets give the best touch.

The blind, bony cat still snuggles and purrs.
Mind ruined, my grandfather regressed, touch

the only language he still understood.
The daycare worker craves a rest from touch.

One ivy vine spread to swallow the hedges.
Glances and flirty words progressed to touch.

When the veteran trembles, his wife knows – lift
his shirt. Her hands warm, each scar caressed – touch

brings him home. A hand-squeeze, a hug, a back
massage comfort. But – slap, shove, grabbed breast – touch

also brings infinite shades of pain. K
was never exposed, never confessed. Touch

he may have long-forgotten marks her still.
Close-up of the actress's large chest: *Touch* –

a toucha toucha half-dressed Janet sings.
Frankie's creature acts at her behest – *Touch*

me. In lucky beds, lips fat from kissing,
crotches sore, red marks where fingers pressed – touch –

satiated lovers slumber. Posed in
a rowboat in December, hair messed, touch

of blush, the model pretends the camera
is a hand. Lets herself be undressed. *Touch*

someone, urges the phone company ad.
Given a chance, the nerd impressed with touch.

Gulls squabble over scraps while noon sun burns
unwary worshipers. Waves swell, crest, touch

the shoreline only as they peter out.
In latex gloves, the doctors dressed for touch.

Praise, Stone, the lonely souls who don't give up,
who haunt bars and parks in a quest for touch.

Friendly Ghazal

To kids, it matters who has the most friends.
New England jokes lost on our West Coast friends.

Sunny and hailing, the sky can't decide.
They were drunken lovers, now almost-friends.

Romance versus reputation. Do you
prep more for a blind date or to host friends?

The day wasted, night comes down like a fist.
He drinks vodka alone, then with ghost friends.

Your horrendous date, your fantasies, your
fears. How no one *liked* your witty post – friends

listen. Middle-age feeds on memory –
teen love, that summer on the coast with friends.

Halloween lets secret selves emerge. Those
muscle-suited heroes? Your Milquetoast friends.

My Russian students call sugar *White Death*.
We raise plastic cups and toast – *To friends*.

During this contemporary plague, no
exodus, no blood on the doorpost. Friends

kept apart. Stone misses handclasps, hugs, the
chance to commiserate and boast with friends.

Less Stern

Is that a crocus? Do I discern spring?
Where does middle-age fancy turn in spring?

Death claims every season. Uncle sickened
in summer. We took home his urn in spring.

Fluffing the pillows, baking bread, Ceres
readies for her daughter's return. In spring,

toes come out of hiding. So many shades
of green polish – Forest, Cool Mint, Fern, Spring.

In winter, I journey by the Hanged Man's
hidden sun. The Hermit's lantern in spring.

Woken at five by an explosion of
birdsong, I crave a more taciturn spring.

What you cling to will be taken is the
lesson of fall. *Still-hopeful hearts yearn* – spring.

Safe to step out hatless, bare-armed. Linger
in noon light. Warmth without the burn in spring.

Cherry trees' pink blossoms hint at mercy.
The visage of stone gods less stern in spring.

Heaven

Brought back to life, she claimed she'd seen heaven.
The vast, dazzling machine of heaven.

Jews believe that you need all your pieces.
Christians can rise without limbs, spleen – Heaven

provides. Sea-loving uncle, I dream you
casting nets in a fish-jeweled green heaven.

Bodies writhe as a disco ball spews stars.
Furtive key bumps. Stamped on glassine – *Heaven,*

Poison, dice. Martyrs' bones hang on walls.
The unbaptized hover between heaven

and flame. My daughter says, *That's a mood.* Teens
pose online, seraphim preen in heaven.

Many flavors of bliss. Introverts say,
Sorry to miss the party, mean *Heaven's*

a lap cat, a book. Loss follows beauty.
The stillborn babe wouldn't wean from heaven.

Harsh hospital light. The screen flatlines. She's
raised by pale hands of morphine to heaven.

Earth's messy with sex and blood. Burning off
all but purity, hell's pristine. Heaven's

claimed by the Pope – Hera demoted to
fable, Mary the new Queen of Heaven.

Stone wants coziness – kids' scribbles and pet
hair. Not a glossy magazine heaven.

Truth

Things that bite – a wounded tomcat, thyme, truth.
Nostalgia's rag can wipe the grime from truth.

A woman can't be unraped or a corpse
revived. The best we get after crime, truth.

At twelve, her vocation is starvation.
Her friends like makeovers, movies, slime, Truth

or Dare. She wants mastery, freedom from
the flesh. Transcendence, not some small-time truth.

He pines for the one who left, recalls hot,
frequent sex, strolls through the Guggenheim. Truth

redacted by his loneliness. Nights we
chase the dragon's tail toward the sublime, truth

evident and able to be shouldered.
In morning's crass, vindictive light, I'm truth-

slapped, worn. Waiting for a savior or a sign
of something better. In the meantime, truth

does what it does. Is life so simple – Make
a ladder of your breath and climb toward truth?

The beggar stops us, sing-songing, *I charge
two bucks for flattery, a dime for truth.*

A slick fib can open legs or doors, make
talk easy when there isn't time for truth.

Poisoned barbs cloaked in honesty hit their
marks. We need a new paradigm for truth.

Hearing mars the melody, Stone learned
from Keats. Beauty, not fact, should rhyme with truth.

Part 3

Split

The body susses lies the mind believes.
Clench in the shoulders, flutter in the chest.
Will we listen? Go when it's time to leave?

A con artist cons. A spider weaves.
Though vows are spoken, loyalty professed,
the body susses lies. Dumb mind believes

a pair of pretty lips. Slick words deceive.
The first slight or slap offers a test
that hurts to pass. *Go when it's time to leave,*

our gut instructs, but hard to cleave
from love gone stale or dangerous. Undressed,
the body susses lies the mind believes.

We cling like autumn's final stubborn leaves,
spin ruin into *It's all for the best.*
The body susses lies the mind believes,
but we don't heed. Stay when it's time to leave.

Twist

A gopher hole. One careless step. Keen pain.
I crumple to the ground, sprawl among
weeds. Ankle won't hold me. Feels like a sprain.

Ice. Compression. Advil. Ice again.
Rest. Ice cream. Hope I won't be laid up long.
Forced idleness is worse than pain.

Entire week of plans goes down the drain.
I struggle with the crutches, get it wrong.
Inner weather's cloudy. Feels like rain.

Enough! My stoicism starts to wane.
Self-pity croons its sweet, familiar song
of missteps, loss, and childhood pain.

Now I'm upgraded to a cane.
Like an old woman, I shuffle along.
Death feels closer. I start prayin'

but fear is not devotion. I can't feign
belief, can only struggle, lurch along
uneven earth. Press forward through the pain.
My faith feels broken. Hope it's just a sprain.

There's Still

There's still aliveness left for us to share,
though autumn days are cold and getting colder.
We met at school in France. Can't go back there.

Decades since you approached me on a dare,
a heart inked on your arm, snake on your shoulder.
There's still aliveness left for us to share.

Even rebels fall into time's snare –
gray, thick-waisted, shrinking, each day older.
We met at school in France. Can't go back there.

Was our last fight over cats? Sex? Silverware?
Allowed a re-do, I'd be bolder.
There's still aliveness left for us to share.

I reach to you with words. Longing laid bare.
Write back. Tell me banked embers smolder
though we're far from France, can't go back there.

My two marriages, your three, went nowhere.
Do your regrets begin, *I used to hold her?*
There's still aliveness left for us to share.
We loved at school in France. Let's go back there.

Choiceless Villanelle

How fragile – heart, brain, womb, sinew, and bone.
How easily bodies, and dreams, can die.
A woman's safest when she is alone.

Witch, in the name of Jesus Christ atone!
Protesters raise bloodstained dolls up high.
Soreness in heart, brain, womb, sinew, and bone.

Preyed upon as maiden, scorned as crone.
Carved up by men's gaze to breast and thigh,
a woman's safest when she is alone.

Listen! How the stunted daughters groan
from laws that quell, relationships that tie
the heart, control brain, womb, sinew, and bone.

Unless her words and organs are her own,
liberty for all's a flag-wrapped lie.
A woman's safest when she is alone.

From preachers in glass houses rocks are thrown.
Hair rearranged by wind, beneath a sky
whose blue drapes heart, brain, womb, sinew, and bone,
a woman's safest when she is alone.

I Love You, Stormy Daniels
(a tanka)

Sweet the cuffs will close
due to a porn star he said
looks like his daughter.

Cops got Capone for taxes,
too. Who's grabbed by the crotch now?

Haiku

Held in the night sky
of your body after love –
half-moons of my nails

News

It's not the billy-club, it's the motion.
Spilled oil chokes ocean
dwellers. Regret is a masturbatory emotion.

Children taunt the caged ape.
Aggressive seagulls ruin picnics at Cape
Cod. What will happen when our ids escape?

Adam lost a rib, Van Gogh an ear.
Vodka puts a leash on fear.
Earth's an ellipse, not a sphere.

What can cure, can ail.
There's a dead mother in every fairy tale,
have you noticed? Poor Freud's gone stale.

Neighbors' sex lives enter through the vent.
What you can't prevent,
devour. There's a hero for every event.

There's a cold shoulder for every ache.
A trashed hotel every spring break.
Six wounded women for every rake.

Better to make art than to create
drama. On a scale of one to ten, please rate
your heart. It's tattooed with the words you ate.

Snowflake

You judge me fragile, weak,
too humorless or slow
to get the joke 'cause I turn up my kale-
adoring, East Coast nose
at your meme about the diplomat, fake
teeth, fat showgirls, and a snake.
I restrain myself, for blood's sake
don't mock your spelling *hoes* like lawn-
care tools. Maybe I do crave a *safe*
space, somewhere light bouncing off snow
or women's tears jolts everyone awake.

Parental

Gone, sweet hours I'd plant
kisses on your silky nape
and you'd clutch my breast with petal-
soft hands. Because you didn't have to earn
my love, you scorn it now, tear
off my fingers as if they burned. Aren't
we every mother/daughter, each playing her part?
I, outworn, discarded, learn-
ing that your adoration was just rent-
ed from time. You, a self apart
from me, pushing me down as you leap
away to prove you're real.

Shameful

Tied to memory's leash,
you heel but never heal,
triggered back to that same
shame as past and present fuse.
Never forgiven, never safe,
you have no self
beyond this dumb mule-
stubborn loyalty, the lash
of each belief your lame
will offered up for sale.

Therapy

Pain's many shapes – abandonment, rape,
Dad drunk or absent, Mom a harpy.
Blighted crops of childhood you reap
and reap. You're a wolf in a trap,
or the past is a wolf and you're prey.
Failed, repetitive relationships, a heap
of half-lived year-
s. Finally, pulsing with fear and hope, tear-
s falling, you risk what you hate
to talk about but must. The heart
exposed before an Other, part
confessor, part good pare-
nt (nonjudgmental, rapt)
who will encourage but not pry
and, when you speak the worst things, hear.

Passover

Faith's needed for the parts we can't prove –
an angel's guiding hand, the soap
opera of jealous brothers, asps
magicked from staffs. We parse
miracles as the seder goes into over-
time. Though we have a lot to rave
about – a prophet sent to save
us from slavery, our first-borns spare-
d – there's Easter candy envy as we serve
herbs dipped in salt water and pass
flat bread. An egg-laying rabbit's poes-
y. Wandering in the desert's prose.

Say Her Name

Say, mind on your new job, you change lanes, don't signal,
And a cop sees you, his skin white and thin,
N-words stashed in his heart the way a perp hides
Drugs. Asked to snuff your smoke, you know your
Rights. Question history about how far that gets you.
Ask the holstered gun.

Because there are no witnesses, we'll never
Learn exactly when or how
A plastic bag that shouldn't be there finds your
Neck. A tragedy but not a crime, they say. You can't
Disagree or finger anyone.

Suburban Development

Our streets had the names of old-fashioned girls –
Nancy, Claudette, Agnes. Each house the same.
Fathers taught their sons to mow the small lawns.
Girls galloped on brooms, fed dolls plastic milk.
Mrs. Polansky passed out on our couch.
My brother's friend fell off his bike and died.
Mom cried, then never said his name again.
Is Bishop right that someone loves us all?

You had to eat everything on your plate.
When finished, *May I be excused?*
No TV at dinner except during the playoffs.
Football time lied – two minutes dragged for twelve.
Longing to be somewhere else,
I starved myself to safety, transcendence.

***

I starved myself to safety, transcendence,
skin pale as the angels I imagined.
Did angels start as humans and then die?
Ann Stevens had a problem with her lungs.
She was skinny but still came to Brownies.
Then an ambulance parked in her driveway
and her parents and sister moved away.
My parents acted like she went with them.

One evening on TV – A Case of Rape.
The ad blared, *The first time she told no one.*
The raped woman used to star in Bewitched.
People kept saying that it was her fault.
She couldn't twitch her nose and make things change.
Each birthday I wished that magic was real.

***

Each birthday I wished that magic was real.
Otherwise, making wishes was pointless.
Tarot cards, Ouija board, ESP book,
trying to move a pencil with my will.
No luck. I was stuck in the mundane world,
with friends who left. With arguments and chores.
My brother got outside, I got kitchen.
Any fool could see it was a bum deal.

Were kitchens the reason women were so mad?
Outside had breezes and the neighbors' cats.
Meals had to be planned, cooked, served, then cleaned up.
Mom was always the last one to sit down.
No one waited for her to begin eating.
The dog left when anger started to spill.

***

The dog left when anger started to spill.
I knew what night it was by the TV.
We watched the detective shows that Dad liked –
Kojak's bald head shiny as Farrah's teeth.
Being shot at didn't mean you would die.
Some episodes men slapped their girlfriends,
then everything was ok and they kissed.
That was dating. Marriage was the dishes.

We wore braids with plastic bows, shorts under
our dresses in case someone pulled them up.
There were five girls on my street so someone
always had to be the person left out.
For favors, we'd say, *I'll be your best friend.*
We were lying, of course. Everyone knew.

***

We were lying, of course. Everyone knew
there were secrets under the tablecloths,
the makeup. In the trunk of the new car.
I envied Sue her family's honest mess.
Her parents were the only divorced ones.
None of the other mothers had to work
for money and not join the PTA.
Sue was strong so no one teased her.

Ropes hung from the gym ceiling like huge worms.
Even if I burned my hands, I only
got a couple inches up, then dropped.
It would have been nice to enter the sky.
Sue was the only girl to reach the top.
The rest of us watched – earthbound, envious.

***

The rest of us watched – earthbound, envious
while astronauts got to visit the moon.
We saw the moon on nights we went outside.
We could see stars, too. Or were they airplanes?
I couldn't figure out what to wish on.
That was even before we learned some stars
are dead, and also that our bodies are
made from them. Do siblings get the same stars?

They didn't get the same anything else.
Dad hated Mom's friend Harriet because
she was a Women's Libber, with short hair
and a laugh that filled the room.
She talked about changing things, which scared me.
Whenever my life changed, something was lost.

***

Whenever my life changed, something was lost.
Each time a friend moved, I watched more TV.
Nixon declared that he wasn't a crook.
I had liked him because he did something
with pandas that made the news anchors smile.
The bears meant China wasn't mad at us.
A Cuban family moved onto our street.
They weren't Communist, so it was ok.

Lisa and I were obsessed with horses,
play ones we had and the real ones waiting.
Then Lisa's father's shoe business *took off*
and she moved to a big house with a barn.
I still saddled and cantered my plastics,
but sadness leaked out from beneath the game.

***

Sadness leaked out from beneath the games played
on fields or boards, in parents' bedrooms.
Sometimes Mom and Dad were mad and didn't
speak to one another. *Tell your father
dinner's ready.   Ask Mom to pass the salt.*
Then they went back to talking but the air
was charged. I got a lot of stomachaches.
Being sick meant you could nap on the couch,
watch TV all day, and eat popsicles.

When I had a fever I'd watch, then doze,
half-seen plots mixing in with my dreams.
If I needed something, I rang a bell.
Mom was sweet unless I stayed sick too long.
Then she got scared and snapped, *Stop coughing.*
I had to pretend that I was OK.

***

I had to pretend that I was OK,
not talk about the boys who followed me home
and knocked the books from my hands.
They smirked and made noises about my new body.
Jill had breasts, too, and kept a thick vest in
her desk. We took turns wearing it to hide.
Then Jill dumped me for Liz Barrista,
who looked like a boy and wore ugly shoes.

What you wore didn't matter at all, then
suddenly it did. Izod shirts and boys'
jeans or corduroys from expensive stores,
not bargain Levis with their tags cut out.
The rules for what was OK kept changing.
It was important not to make mistakes.

***

It was important not to make mistakes,
or else you'd be picked last for teams in gym
and no one would let you sit down at lunch.
You couldn't be fat or brainy or poor,
or different, unless you were popular
like Ellen. Her freckles blurred together
like orange ink. Stuttering, stooped-over
Jane had freckles, too, but hers were ugly.

Dad said that someone's looks shouldn't matter,
but he talked about cute blondes and pointed
them out to my brother. When one walked by,
Mom's lips got thinner and she looked
like she might say something but then didn't.
There was always something not being said.

***

There was always something not being said,
someone's throat closed tight around the hidden
things that we were not supposed to notice.
If you did notice, you had to shut up.
That was the most important rule. Once, to see
what would happen, I told about being touched.
Mom laughed shrilly and Dad changed the subject
to drugged-out boys with long hair burning flags.

I couldn't know what Dad's job was, just that
he had a high security clearance
and flew to cities with exotic names.
Mom got nervous when generals came
for dinner. I'd help her scoop out melon balls,
fold napkins, and put out the fancy plates.

***

Cloth napkins and fancy plates didn't help
when conversations started to boil.
Mom and Dad told us racism's wrong but
laughed when Uncle Richard told *Polack* jokes.
There was one Chinese kid in my class, Steve
Chang. No Black kids till a program bused some
in. Then the program ended and they left.

A few of us were Jewish, but we sang
the Christmas songs, so it wasn't a big deal.
We pledged *One nation, indivisible*
until the school board added *under God,*
which made my parents mad. They liked God, but
some things needed to be kept separate.

***

Some things needed to be kept separate,
like boys' and girls' sports teams, like Church and State.
When school started a minute of silence
for prayer or meditation, parents
who thought God belonged in church
told their kids to get up and sharpen
pencils. I was supposed to be one of
the pencil kids, but I liked the quiet.

When it was quiet I could look around
and watch people tap fingers or eat their hair.
The sharpener got full. Did anyone know
what prayers we were supposed to say?
The teachers didn't care. What mattered was
appearances, not truths our bodies knew.

***

Appearances, not truths my body knew,
controlled how I acted. Everyone was
controlled by something. I could see the strain
in my parents' eyes, hear the fear behind
the cool girls' jokes. No one wanted to
not get invited or to be the one
always made *It*. Boys could sometimes be
honest, hit other boys and make them bleed.

Most families had two children. Some had three.
When Ann died, her parents only had one.
Each house had the same-sized yard, with tulips
and a swing set. You could choose the colors.
Children shot baskets in driveways or played
on streets with the names of old-fashioned girls.

***

Where streets had the names of old-fashioned girls,
I starved myself to safety, transcendence,
each birthday wishing that magic was real.
The dog left when anger started to spill.
We were often lying. Everyone knew.
Rockets launched as we watched – earthbound, envious.
Whenever my life changed, something was lost,
and sadness lurked beneath the games we played.

I had to pretend that I was OK.
It was important not to make mistakes,
or to let slip the things not being said
near the folded napkins and fancy plates.
Some things needed to be kept separate –
appearances from truths our bodies knew.

***

Part 4

Shelter in Place

Crocus, snowdrop, daffodil. Expanding light.
Yards hedged by forsythia, yellow as
the Caution tape blocking off the playground.
No squeals of children, murmurings of moms.

Yards hedged by forsythia. *Yellow* as
slur – *cowardly*. Attacks on Asian-Americans.
Squeals of children, murmurings of moms
as school becomes the kitchen table.

Slurs. Attacks on Asian-Americans.
There must be someone to blame.
School becomes the kitchen table.
Today's lesson: fear. Tomorrow's: death.

There must be someone to blame.
Nurses wear bandanas or garbage bags.
Today's lesson: fear. Tomorrow's: death.
For distraction, we watch movies. Take walks.

Nurses wear bandanas or garbage bags.
On the news, a curve, climbing higher.
For distraction we watch movies. Take walks,
praise what we can.

On the news, a curve climbing higher,
Caution tape blocking off playgrounds.
Still, we praise what we can –
crocus, snowdrop, daffodil. Expanding light.

Quarantine Morning

What are the songbirds saying,
loud outside my window as I grasp at sleep?
Trees pour shadows onto empty streets.
The air is sweet, the sky clean of machines.

Loud outside my window as I grasp at sleep,
the flagrant magnolia, starting to unpetal.
The air is sweet, sky clean of machines
since people have been forced to pause.

The flagrant magnolia starts to unpetal.
Waxy pink and white carpet, soon to brown.
Since people have been forced to pause,
the moon has shown us all her faces.

Waxy pink and white carpet, soon to brown –
small window between beauty and decay.
The moon has shown us all her faces.
Can we make meaning from the dead stars' light?

Small window between beauty and decay.
Trees pour shadows onto empty streets.
What is the meaning of the dead stars' light?
What are the songbirds saying?

Quarantine Beltane

Hey, ho, make a merry din!
Weaving over, under, laughing at mess-ups,
we circled, flowers in our hair,
ribbons chosen to match our desires.

Weaving over, under, laughing at mess-ups –
Past Beltanes had hugs and
ribbons chosen to match our desires.
This May brings a different choreography.

Past Beltanes had hugs,
shared food, a goblet passed around.
This May brings a different choreography,
fear of what breath spreads along with song.

Shared food, a goblet passed around.
My favorite holiday.
Fearing what breath spreads along with song,
now we must reach for the sacred from separate houses.

My favorite holiday asserts –
Days will lengthen, sun's full strength return,
though we must reach for the sacred from separate houses.
Whatever humans do, the earth keeps turning.

Days will lengthen, sun's full strength return,
though we can't circle with flowers in our hair.
Whatever humans do, the earth keeps turning.
Summer is a comin' in.

Something More

There's always something more that can be lost.
Locked down, I drift through blended days,
drag the dog on yet another walk.
Six weeks have passed. Or is it seven?

Locked down, I drift through blended days.
My older daughter's bored enough to bond.
Six weeks have passed. Or is it seven?
What if we're just postponing tragedy?

My older daughter's bored enough to bond.
For diversion, we watch handsome actors in a hospital –
Often, the doctors just postpone tragedy.
Dying patients alternate with sex scenes.

Mindless diversion – handsome actors in a hospital
where bodies pile up like rocks.
Dying patients alternate with sex scandals
in the news I hate but can't turn off.

Bodies pile up like rocks.
The lungs of parents, spouses, children fail
in the news I hate but can't turn off.
Near-empty streets are petal-splotched.

Parents, husband, daughters, son,
the dog I drag on yet another walk –
(Near-empty streets are petal-splotched.)
There's always something more that can be lost.

Mnemonic Pantoum

Hospital, pet, concert, third grade crush.
How is it decided which memories last,
which fade like Krazy Kolor from a punk teen's hair?
I'll never forget the beagle shot in *Daddles*.

How is it decided which memories last?
Advertising jingles edge out family members.
I'll never forget the beagle shot in *Daddles*
or my teacher's one green/one brown eyes.

Advertising jingles edge out family members.
There's not enough heart-room for everything.
My teacher's one green/one brown eyes
watched us wash chalk from the blackboard.

There's not enough heart-room for everything.
Time takes back some joy, some shame,
the way children wash chalk from a blackboard.
Hyperthymesiacs remember every second of their lives.

Time takes back some joy, some shame.
We're left with just a smattering of heightened scenes,
though hyperthymesiacs remember every second of their lives –
each meal, each beach, each late-night conversation.

We're left with a smattering of heightened scenes,
vibrant as Krazy Kolor in a punk teen's hair –
that meal, that beach, that late-night conversation.
Hospital, pet, concert. Third grade crush.

One to Keep

Allowed only one memory, which would you choose?
Alzheimer's-stricken, my grandfather kept his store –
smell of sawdust, the walls' exact gray.
His wife and daughters a daily surprise.

Alzheimer's-stricken, my grandfather kept his store,
his attention fixed on long-dead customers.
His wife and daughters a daily surprise.
Do we retain what we know best, or love the most?

Attention fixed on what's long-dead,
many of us miss today's light.
Do we retain what we know best, or love the most?
Sometimes things are taken anyway.

Many of us miss today's light,
grieving what we've lost to the pandemic.
Sometimes things are taken
despite our clinging and rage.

As we grieve what we've lost to the pandemic,
the air cleans and animals claim space.
Despite our clinging and rage,
humans have been forced from places we took.

The air's cleaner. Animals claim space.
Buffalo on beaches, elk in yards –
Humans forced from places we took.
When businesses reopen, these images will fade.

Buffalo on beaches, elk in yards.
Smell of sweetgrass, each rock's exact gray.
When businesses reopen, these images will fade.
Allowed to keep one memory, which would you choose?

Many Shades

Lost loves never finish disappearing.
His eyes' specific brown, her laugh's low notes –
Even our memories break down like worn cassettes.
There are so many shades of *gone.*

His eyes' specific brown, her laugh's low notes
come back now in dreams or not at all.
There are so many shades of *gone.*
The world stitches itself around the wound.

Come back now, even in dreams! Not all
shells held to the ear bring oceans close.
The world stitches itself around our wounds.
These days hold new voices, new flowers.

Can shells held to the ear bring oceans close,
though the old wooden beach house rotted?
These days hold new voices, new flowers.
Forks in roads show – something must be chosen.

The old wooden beach house rotted.
Bathing suits outgrown, old selves sloughed off
at forks in roads. Something must be chosen,
something pushed aside and named *the past.*

Bathing suits outgrown, old selves sloughed off.
Even our memories break down like worn cassettes.
Pushed aside and named *the past,*
lost loves never finish disappearing.

Poem Inspired by a Line by Natalie Diaz

I submit to mystery, then I become it.
A half-heard phrase compels more than a clear command.
Who's fool enough to protest when the forest calls,
all that darkness and moon-made shadow.

A half-heard phrase compels more than a clear command.
We follow, as our blood dictates.
All that darkness and moon-made shadows
offer us, we want, at least once.

We follow as our blood dictates.
Ecstasy and oblivion tease with the same release,
offer us what we want. At least once,
every timid heart admits its cravings.

Ecstasy and oblivion tease with the same release.
Lovers long for boundaries to dissolve.
Even timid hearts can admit cravings.
There is no joy without surrender.

Lovers long for boundaries to dissolve,
a vacation from the dusty self.
There is no joy without surrender,
no thrill without the slap of the new.

A vacation from the dusty self
leaves me wanting more –
more thrill with the slap of the new,
more midnight and strange rustlings.

Left wanting more,
I'm Fool enough to go when the forest calls
at midnight with strange rustlings.
I submit to mystery, then I become it.

House

Childhood's a house of slanted rooms
at the intersection of nostalgia and pain.
Has the spirit nowhere better to live?
The heart's a predictable fist.

At the intersection of gender and pain,
girls learn disgust for their bodies.
The heart's a predictable fist –
Open. Clench. Hungry, alive until not.

Girls learn disgust for their bodies,
heavy vessels of flesh that
open, clench. Hungry and alive until not.
You can't stay safe there, can't really leave.

Heavy vessel of memories,
the past takes so much attention.
You can't stay safe there, can't really leave.
What's incomplete pursues us everywhere.

The past takes so much attention,
why has the spirit nowhere better to live?
What's incomplete pursues us. Everywhere,
childhood's house of slanted rooms.

NOTES

Sometimes the Eyes are Enough
The first line takes an image from Emily Dickinson.

Poem Inspired by a Line by Natalie Diaz
The first and last line borrow, and alter, Diaz's line: "I obey what I
  don't understand, then I become it."

GRATITUDES

To my first teachers – Hugo Williams, who convinced me to switch
from fiction, and the late Allen Grossman, whose generosity lasted
years after I graduated.

To the wonderful poets and readers of my online communities –
John Adames, Noelle Canin, Heather Ferguson, Karen Alkalay-Gut,
Robert Priest, Carolyn Smart, and The One O'clock Poets. My work
is better because of your insights and feedback.

To Raymond Hammond and everyone at NYQ Books. You're a pleasure to work with and I'm delighted my book found such a wonderful home.

To the family and friends who, via phone, Zoom, and far-apart walks,
made pandemic living less lonely and more fun.

Michael, Jessy, and Vee, if I had to quarantine with anyone, I'd pick
you.

Acknowledgments

Thanks to the editors of the following publications where these poems first appeared, some in other versions or with different titles:

The Bezine: Say Her Name
Diode: Poem Inspired by a Line by Natalie Diaz
Earth's Daughters: There's Still, Picket Fence
First of the Month: December, Tactile Ghazal, Truth, Well-Lit, Hungry Ghazal, Road to Ruin, What's Seen, Choiceless Villanelle, Monsters, Bees, Desires, Time, After Hours, Inspired by a Line by Janis, Like the Night, Into the Woods, Quarantine Beltane
First Literary Review East: Passover, Weeds
Folio: The Plan
Global Poemic: New York April, 2020
Gyroscope Review: Teen Pantoum, Louder than Laughter
Iconoclast: Lost Ghazal, Sometimes the Eyes are Enough
The Lake (UK): House, Pantoum with an Idea Borrowed from Lisa Rhoades
New York Quarterly: Visit, Yourself
Poetry International: Haiku
RHINO: Enough about You
San Pedro River Review: Rocky Horror Pantoum, Many Shades, How Louisa May Alcott is Similar to God
Shot Glass Journal: Snowflake
SoFloPoJo: Time Pantoum, Suburban Development (titled Neighborhood of Make-Believe)
Spectrum Literary Journal: Say Her Name
Steam Ticket: April Ghazal
The Wild Word: Cargo

Shelter in Place appeared in the anthology *The Power of the Pause* (Wising Up Press, 2022)

103

ABOUT THE AUTHOR

Alison Stone is the author of eight other full-length collections, *To See What Rises* (CW Books, 2023), *Zombies at the Disco* (Jacar Press, 2020), *Caught in the Myth* (NYQ Books, 2019), *Dazzle* (Jacar Press, 2017), *Masterplan*, a book of collaborative poems with Eric Greinke (Presa Press, 2018), *Ordinary Magic* (NYQ Books, 2016), *Dangerous Enough* (Presa Press, 2014), and *They Sing at Midnight*, which won the 2003 Many Mountains Moving Poetry Award; as well as three chapbooks. Her poems have appeared in *The Paris Review, Poetry, Ploughshares, Barrow Street, Poet Lore,* and many other journals and anthologies. She has been awarded *Poetry*'s Frederick Bock Prize, the *New York Quarterly*'s Madeline Sadin Award, and *The Lyric*'s Lyric Poetry Prize. She was Writer in Residence at LitSpace St. Pete. She is also a painter and the creator of The Stone Tarot. A licensed psychotherapist, she has private practices in NYC and Nyack. https://alisonstone.info Youtube and TikTok – Alison Stone Poetry.